Have you *ever* wondered if aliens exist?

Are they like humans?

Which living being on Earth do aliens most want to talk to?

How do they bring up kids?

Do they pay taxes? Is there an alien religion?

What are Fermions, and why are they so vital to the universe?

Poet-translator Steve Cranfield and multi-media artist Andrea Aste have been authorised by the Alien Assembly to bring you the answers to these questions, and many more.

By Steve Cranfield

Prospero's Cave: Recollections of Peter Forster (poems)
Keats's Anchovy (poems)
Salt and Honey, with Martin Humphries (poems)
De purísimo azul / Of Purest Blue, Selected Poems of
    Francisco Brines, with Claudio Tedesco (translation)
F. R. Leavis: The Creative University (criticism)

www.stevecranfield.co.uk

Alien Poetry

First published in 2023 by Anchovy Verse, London UK

978-1-7399301-2-7

Cover, art, and book design by Andrea Aste
www.andreaaste.co.uk

Acknowledgement

Thanks are due to the Alien Assembly for its kind permission to include reproductions of the original logical alphabet.

Alien Poetry

Translated by
Steve Cranfield
Art Reproduced by
Andrea Aste

Contents

To Piotr Drukier
Wise Alien

Homo sum, humani a me nihil alienum puto
I am a human being, nothing human is alien to me

Terence, *The Self-Tormentor*

One of the first and still most significant achievements of the alien civilisation has been the development of a huge logical alphabet to facilitate communication between species. When aliens first made contact with one another, tools of communication and expression tended to be ad hoc: one alien grunted, the other gesticulated; one emitted magnetic waves, the other produced visual images; one released odours and inks, the other gave off electric sparks; and so on. The parties fumbled towards mutual enlightenment as best they might.

In those far-off days the odds of an alien civilisation reaching a certain age, making it more likely it would receive a probe or visit from another – the so-called 'Contact Era'[1] – were very low. With an abundance of alien civilisations eventually entering the fray, the length of the Contact Era – previously of the order of hundreds if not thousands of years (to use sidereal terms) – was greatly reduced. The stage was reached that made a convenient tool for common communication an ever more urgent goal.

Hence, the logical alphabet. This makes it possible to translate any given medium of communication into any other: sounds into smells; smells into visual images; visual images into sounds; and so on, with practically 100% fidelity. This book contains some specimen reproductions of the logical alphabet in a two-dimensional visual format

[1] Amri Wandel (2022) 'The Fermi Paradox Revisited: Technosignatures and the Contact Era', *The Astrophysical Journal*, 941(2), 184.

suitable for the written page or digital display screen. These examples have been redrawn from originals supplied by the Alien Assembly to the artist Andrea Aste and can be consulted alongside the accompanying translations into English grunts by the poet Steve Cranfield.

Readers may deduce that the alphabet appears to combine images and glyphs reminiscent of Earthling picture-languages such as Mayan. However, the alien alphabet does not denote single objects or concepts. To go some way towards indicating its scope and properties we can do no better than call on the apt, elegant expression of the Earthling linguist Otto von Weissnichtwo, when he says that each glyph represents a 'cognitive galaxy … which could contain Goethe's entire *Faust*!'[2]

Of course, how does one unpack something as rich and fantastic as *Faust*, let alone a single glyph of the alien alphabet, in just a few pages? Choices must be made, but which? 'Traduttore, traditore' ('translator, traitor') — the Italian language pinpoints the issue at stake here in its typically musical way. How much of the authentic alien galaxy has made it intact and unadulterated to the English text and reproductions in your hand? Think of this book as a battery or conductor of energy. Conventional poetry is written in artificial forms which often mean that the original impulse or charge is destroyed. Nothing *real* is left for the reader, the distinctly alien perspective on galactic life is lost. This book is different. Discussions with

---

[2] Some readers will note echoes of the work of other leading Earth linguists such as Professor Noam Chomsky, University of Arizona, and notably of Professor Elettra Scintilla, the Sapienzia University of Rome.

Cranfield and Aste, our representatives on Earth, have made it a central commitment of their task to calibrate the form and content to ensure that the maximum of energy is transmitted and in as compact and comprehensible a way as possible. Even so, we welcome feedback on the translations, which may be sent through environmentally-friendly smoke signals, flashing lights trained on the night sky (provided these do not trigger adverse physical reactions) or via the email address below.

One of the prime aims of this book is the reduction of fear, fear of the other, fear of the unknown, fear even of poetry itself. Be assured that we aliens have your best interests at heart. We are not here to spook you. As we explain in the introductory poem, 'Our words will be ones you are at home in'. It is hoped that readers will accept these translations as some sort of acknowledgement, however inadequate, of the gift to humanity of the extraordinary body of alien wisdom.

Source:
Alien Conclave on Translation
978-1-7399301-2-7
Orion-Cygnus Arm of the Milky Way
Updated 2023

alienconclave@gmail.com

If aliens are prodigies of intelligence,
it's not that we're eggheads, illuminati,
pondering life in theory and the abstract;
rather, we're like busy commercial playwrights,
preoccupied with making life stageable.

And if aliens are creatives in demand,
it's not because we like to throw the dice
of our being to see where it happens to fall,
on nothing and nowhere in particular.
No alien trades on empty promises.

And if we are not waltzing nonchalantly
along a narrow plank, whistling the while,
this does not mean we are not partial to
booby traps, pratfalls and banana skins,
and, most prized of all, the vanishing act.

We strive to be instantly understood
by finicky, distracted audiences,
creatures of modest ambition, ever vexed
by money and debt, harassed by diseases,
hunger, yearnings. Creatures like you, in fact.

Any knowledge we deem safe to impart
to you from time to time will be adapted
to your particular needs and circumstances.
In this, we will be answerable only
to our own finely-tuned consciences.

Hence, there is no need for you to worry
about the languages we might adopt
to communicate with you. Aliens
adjust themselves to speech communities.
Our words will be ones you are at home in.

And if we invite you on an excursion,
it will be in a conveyance of your choosing,
with ample legroom, excellent suspension.
The journey will be one you haven't to pay for.
A 'Thanks for the ride' will be more than enough.

'We aliens …': some sigh when they hear this phrase;
others get riled – 'As if we're all peas in a pod.'
While it's true all aliens have a vote in the Assembly,
in terms of attributes, what aliens have in common
is defined more in terms of negatives.

Some cannot smell the perfume of fig trees, for instance,
or easily count past number seven in Basque.
Contrary to expectations, and Cocteau,
some cannot pass through mirrors with rubber gloves on
(without the rubber gloves, some certainly can).

Of course, as more and more planets come into view,
and increased numbers of aliens join the fray,
there's more to be added to what you aren't or can't.
Time to drop the alien label altogether, some say.
But a voice still asks, 'Aren't you curious about the fig?'

'Why do we bother with the Earthlings?'

'Because they are curious.'

'You mean curious to look at?'

'Hardly. No, because *they* are curious.
Show them a mountain, they will climb it.
Present them with the Moon, they will want to see the dark side.
On the quietest of nights they will look under the bed.
They tell obvious lies to see who will believe them.
At the first sign of distress, they will investigate. Usually.'

'And the most curious of all?'

'Give them perfection and they will destroy it.'

'In the interests of their humanity?'

'I suspect that's the least of it.'

'What if?' sounds a tad too pusillanimous.
Let humans suppose aliens have been here
at least before the so-called dawn of humanity.
We've made ourselves at home, so to speak,
even if the décor's uncongenial.
We've witnessed the first creatures crawl from oceans
and gingerly take their first gulp of O_2
in its gaseous, rust-inducing form.
We placed bets on the ones that would make it.
We have been chatting away since time immemorial,
only no humans have yet bothered to tune in.
All other living creatures, past and present,
have had no issues with communications.
Even rocks have sent out ambassadors.
We aliens are on a mission, apparently
one that will take longer than the average time
spent by the redeemable soul in Purgatory,
which is to sit it out for humans to listen up.
Fortunately, for you humans, we are patient,
and there have been signs, albeit brief and fitful,
down the ages, if you exclude the prophets.
When Virginia Woolf said that she heard birds
talking to her in Greek, we thought this
showed distinct signs of promise, except
few took her in the least bit seriously.
When alien hunters train their radio beams
on Proxima Centauri and the like,
we shrug: 'Wrong needle, wrong haystack.'
When humans get excited by the latest crop circle,
we start to wonder, 'Will they ever learn?'
When Voyager 1 was launched in '77,
with its Golden Record 'Sounds of the Earth',
we had to chuckle: 'All that last year's news.'
When the latest aliens movie hits the screens,
we say, 'We have to show this to the kids!'

The monoliths in Kubrick's *2001*
elicited approving murmurs: 'But didn't he know
that this year's colour is assuredly not black?
Plus, we're not crazy about intergalactic zoos.'
When one of us heard that magic phrase
'hidden in plain sight' first pass human lips,
it beamed: 'We're cooking with gas, as Earthlings say.'
As for the human counter-argument gaining ground
that says the proof of intelligent life out there
is the resounding silence, of aliens keeping
well out of the way, we see this not as despair,
but as one further expression of defensive driving.

Planet Claire has pink air
All the trees are red
No one ever dies there
No one has a head

The B-52s

It's true that no one ever dies there.
The law decrees that no one is allowed
to perish on the planet, or give birth —
such is its importance to all aliens
that everyone is steward of its future,
all claims to inheritance are denied.

Hence, the denizens of Claire are among
the most widely travelled of aliens,
their message one that happiness precedes
true understanding. Lives lived within
a narrow scope will often demonstrate
the more joyous aspects of existence.

The wider the scope the less joyous
the demonstration. Pessimistic, perhaps.
And yet, the nomads of Claire assert
that displacement is the key to our hope
of survival, of tolerable existence,
of how we might grasp the idea of home.

When they glimpse the pink sunsets of cities
and deserts on alien globes, they let out
a squeak of gratitude. When they encounter
the red of fall trees in Connecticut
or bottlebrushes in Aotearoa,
it's as if they have come full circle.

It's true also that no one has a head.
All the organs of sense and intellection,
that most others concentrate in one region,
are in them distributed uniformly.
In their opinion, heads are over-rated:
'Look what they lead to!' Thus, they rest their case.

Put to one side the sci-fi fantasies
for a moment. What makes any Earthling
suppose that if aliens landed tomorrow
homo sapiens would be the species
they would want to negotiate with?

One writer, hearing what animal breeders
have to say, suggests it would be cows,
not humans, who'd be first port of call.
Cows take the time to meditate; their horns
are transmitters connecting them to the cosmos.

Cows are confident, grounded creatures,
not given to sudden, violent conniptions.
As reported by Vinciane Despret,
'They go further than us in their reflections'.
If anyone is the genius of the place, it's the cow.

Earthlings: try this analogy for size.
You are the one setting a tentative foot
on alien terrain. Your destination:
Downing Street, the Kremlin, Zhongnanhai,
the White House, or the Élysée Palace.

You are naturally eager to seek out
intelligent life. Who then best to speak to?
Wouldn't you head for the resident cat, or dog,
or in the case of either being compromised,
a mouse, a moth, a spider, or a fly?

Two aliens are discussing Marx and Brecht.

'What gets me most is how their word "alienation"
invariably has a negative cast:
being estranged from aspects of one's nature,
or the emotional entanglement with
what's happening onstage, as if one's feelings
spell an ending to objectivity.
I think it's their languages that are at fault.
Thankfully, semantics do not trip us up.'

'Yes, but these terrestrials have a point,
even if they never stopped to think
what aliens "have done for us". Despite
its benefits, and these are great, we know
all too well the price paid for alienation
(no pun intended), of living at
too great a distance from ourselves too long.
When was the last time you phoned home?'

It's often asked if aliens have a religion.
Of course, they frequently find themselves
in the slightly awkward position of prompting
one's foundation. They arrive at planets, expecting
to be accorded the status of most honoured guest,
and end up being placed on a pedestal,
propitiated, praised or blamed for the fall
of empires or the rise of certain grasses:
the Cortés-in-Tenochtitlan syndrome.
All aliens are taught what happened next.

Hence, aliens, eager not to displace
the native customs, are in the habit
of arriving with the minimum of fuss,
and leaving negligible traces of a visit.

Not that the local beliefs are without
their attractions. Annatā, the doctrine
of the not-self, for instance: what alien,
having encountered so many not-selves
across the galaxies, is not aware
of that? For most aliens, however, this
is the point of departure, not arrival.

What then of the aliens' own beliefs?
Are these not a source of intergalactic friction?

Here they have hit on a cunning solution,
akin to the idea of terrestrial crop rotation.
Each day a different religion is adopted,
but only for that day, and in strict sequence.
Religions are selected from those encountered;
no auto-religions devised from scratch allowed.

Of course, a day may be longer or shorter,
depending on the mode of measurement,
its system solar or sidereal.
Hence, something akin to Buddhism Monday,
Hinduism Tuesday, Jainism Wednesday,
Christianity Thursday (but only in
its Gnostic version), Islam next, and so on.
But only for that day; come stroke of midnight,
or whatever convention of division
applies, the switch over is instant, total.
A minimum of ten is recommended,
subject to regular review: retreats are offered.

This is not some external pose, a type
of impressions management. Each day obliges
its unwavering commitment, the most
intimate manifestation of the alien's self,
no dilettante 'try this on for size'.

And what of those who speak not God at all?
Here too the aliens' wisdom is at work.
Sceptical, agnostic, atheistic days:
those are permitted too, indeed encouraged,
with the subtlest variations in the blend.
Indian notions of absence come in handy:
there is no God here (absence); a God is
not a rose bush (difference); there is no
God yet in the rose bush (non-existence
prior to existence); God is dead
(non-existence following existence);
Godhead is never found in a rose bush
(something that never exists to start with).

Doctrines chosen focus variously on
the near and the far, the here and now

as distinct from the there and then, and pose
either self, no self, a life to come, none such:
any doubts and anxieties entertained
are never harboured long enough
for these to settle into an *idée fixe*.
Likewise, no cocksure certainties hold sway.

What's more, the system fosters empathy.
If an alien seems unduly brusque,
someone will say, 'It's just Andromeda,'
or, 'It's having one of its Sirius moments;
come back tomorrow, you'll see the difference.'

Naturally, this last example raises
the issue of how one alien signals
to another its prevailing belief system.
For conformity in groups is not imposed.
Some have adopted colour codes but this
is by no means universal, given that
the number of faiths outstrips the spectrum
and not all aliens see the same (or any) colour.
Most opt for daily routines that require
the minimum of ritual observance,
so discreet, in fact, that many outsiders
notice hardly any daily changes.

Some philosophers argue that this method
is itself a religion since its goal
is the elevation of truth, a way
of reaching to the stars. But most aliens
calmly dismiss this notion, as they gaze
(or those that have eyes do) into space,
as though disburdened of the earth
on which they happen to be that day,
wearing the timeless expression of a seer.

They take their eye off the ball sometimes,
quite literally in the case of the third rock
from the Sun. The Earth is but one of many
alien duties of care, albeit logged
on a lower category. Still, they missed
the first manned lunar landing, and by months.

The Chichxulub impact that killed the dinosaurs,
the end of the Younger Dryas, or last ice age,
the oceanic overturns and climate change,
the plate tectonics causing massive earthquakes,
these were considered strictly local events
that hardly registered on the alien scale.

Nothing that warranted an escalation
to H.Q., or triggered an alarm
to prompt a swift remedial action.
Potential or actual interference
by beings beyond their home base – that
was another matter, a cause for concern.

All hell broke loose. An inquiry was launched.
Scouts on duty that day got it in the neck.
Recordings of *The Day the Earth Stood Still*
were dusted off, made mandatory viewing,
Michael Rennie's admonishing speech
to the people of Earth to be learned by rote:

'The universe grows smaller every day,
and the threat of aggression by any group,
anywhere, cannot be tolerated.'
A case study and cautionary tale,
entirely due to the alien, not human, factor:
a classic 'never event', one expert said.

Boulevard T is a very wide street
on one of the most popular planets.
Everyone's heard of Boulevard T.
Visitors form the mistaken impression
the T stands for something else, probably
some totally unpronounceable word –

not that the T doesn't present its challenges
for those lacking voiceless consonants,
and this has given rise to a plethora
of signs and symbols, gestures and smells,
instantly recognised, felt or sniffed as
'Meet you down T', 'Wasn't T cool last night!'

But it's always been T, always this wide.
Initially the width was for the traffic;
that was before vehicles became redundant.
There had been talk of letting the place re-wild
then someone came up with the suggestion:
'Let's make it a forum, a place to linger.'

And so the idea took hold of a cosmic *agora*,
open to those who haven't yet joined the club –
'The Intergalactic Theatre Season:
Coming Attractions'. A performance of
The Tempest was an instant hit, with queues
snaking down the street: it ran for months.

'"O brave new world, that has such people in't!"
How often have we felt exactly that!
What a mind! To present so movingly
the ironic and the unironic vision.
If the rest of them are on that wavelength,
the conversation will keep us up all night.'

Do aliens pay any taxes on their goods?
A related question: do aliens collect them?
Everything starts with a vision of the future.
Imagine, or re-imagine the following.
Alien X buys its raw materials
for a chair, and doesn't pay any tax.
Instead, a virtual terminal sends
real-time info to the tax authority.
Virtual terminals respond to thought,
provided this is fully intentional.

When Alien X sells a chair, the buyer
pays a tax that reflects the value added,
again through a virtual terminal.
This system creates an auditable trail
of each of the parties' captured intentions.
Data sent to the tax authority
is used to calculate Alien X's
corporate income tax. All processes
(apart from chair, and customer trying out
the seat for comfort) function instantly.

This is the set-up which the aliens favour.
So the answer to the first question, whether
aliens pay taxes, is Yes — at least
in this example, admittedly simple.
The answer to the second, however, is No.
No one alien collects them. Here, again,
the aliens have reduced to a minimum
any associated burden, while
increasing the likelihood of compliance,
through the cloak of invisibility.

A desire to make contact is nothing new.
Many a call that's hurled into the void
is a cry for help, for direct assistance.
Should, then, an alien come to humans' aid?
It's a decision not to be undertaken lightly.

Screen out those who are clearly psychotic,
conspiracy theorists of various shades,
those yearning desperately for abduction,
woolly-minded souls searching for gurus,
and you have a tiny, genuine residue.

Even here, though, and allowing for triage,
imagine the consequences should an alien
offer a one-to-one or group consultation.
Allowing for best intentions, it could still
become a game any number can play.

But 'Never say never' is some aliens' motto.
The day a message can be recast in terms
that match those of the Golden Ratio,
it's jackpot time: statistically possible;
in practice, largely inconceivable.

Nothing ages faster than a vision of the future.
Aliens don't have them, such visions that is,
outside of put-your-feet-up relaxation:
wall posters, mini-series, school projects,
wacky ideas for buildings, and the like.
Besides, someone's future is inevitably
someone else's past somewhere in space.

Of more interest are visions from the future
and how best to avert or realise them.
Not indulgence in precognition,
or fanciful dreams – not the aliens' style –
but whether they should succumb to or resist
the lure in the offing, the protensive pull,
of cities in air, disaster capitalism.

Some aliens are very hard of hearing,
not through age, trauma or blocked canals,
but because of the differential volume
at which various aliens tend to speak,
those that speak and listen, to begin with.
What is one's whisper, is another's roar.

Thus, 'How was your Cole Porter experience?'
is not someone eliciting the hearer's
opinion about a recent music concert
but a slightly apprehensive inquiry
about testing out a challenging form of liquid:
'How was your cold water experience?'

Amplification makes some aliens quiver;
loop systems, inaccurate; signing shifts
the burden to other organs; text messaging,
too much time. Instead, aliens revel in
cross purposes (if these are harmless). Besides:
'You don't have to hear the farts, though you can smell them.'

Not all aliens reproduce sexually.
Far from it. They run the whole gamut
from interaction of two or more aliens,
to cloning, growing another from body parts
(moulted or severed), to those which spawn once
in their lifetime, or intermittently.

Most poignant of all, however, are those beings
who do not reproduce at all, who have
no ancestors and no inheritors.
Even synthetic creatures come from something.
Exhaustive searches, including of rogue labs,
have so far turned up nothing. They just appear.

They're known collectively as the Knockers,
because they're forever knocking one hundred,
two hundred, four hundred, a thousand,
or some improbable age. Learned folk
refer to them as Oncers, after those lines
in Rilke's Ninth 'Duino Elegy':

'Just once, everything, only for once.
Once and no more. And we, too, once.
And never again.' Though it's fair to add,
they dislike being lumped together
as emblems, mascots or (worse) freaks. Their fate
frees them from all alien anxieties.

They're exempt from hazardous professions,
though some rebel against the kid-glove treatment,
especially being accompanied downstairs,
and some go in for dare-devil stunts
involving trapezes. 'You only live once'
never had a more profound application.

When a Knocker passes (for they aren't immortal),
a universal mourning is observed.
Something uniquely precious vanishes
from alien ken, strangely symbolic,
but not of anything other than itself,
of haeccity, the thisness of all life.

They visit when they are least expected,
creating maximum inconvenience:
minutes before an important deadline,
at the height of a domestic argument,
during vacations, airline check-ins,
or seconds before the punchline of a joke.
Many's the orgasm ruined by bad timing.

Contrary to expectations, they rarely
communicate in complete sentences,
and they flout the rules of prosody.
That's not to say they glory in ungrammar,
poor puns, or speak in forked tongues, either.
They're bemused to be confused with the Muse:
a ruse that's no excuse for bad assonance.

They're not into systems, and express surprise
when a poet attributes to them a vision.
Look at what Yeats, with his wife's connivance,
span out of what was a mere minor tip
about gyrating bodies. (Embarrassing.
All those yarns about spirit guides. Milton
and Homer were models of discretion, tact.)

That led to a public inquiry on 'inspiration'
and a moratorium on sublunary calls.
Some say it's time the lyric ban was lifted
but only on condition that each visit
be restricted to eight earthly days and nights,
and avoid any reference to mediums,
or indeed media, including social.

'Do you spin or rotate?' It's a good question,
and one that aliens often get asked –
it's included on application forms –
since the two types of motion are not
necessarily identical. To wit:
the Red Spot of Jupiter. The planet
spins on its axis and makes a rotation
of 360 degrees before
the Red Spot – voilà! – appears again.
Most aliens behave likewise: one spin
equals one complete rotation, before
the distinguishing features come into view.

A few, however, have to rotate *twice*,
though 720 degrees,
for things to look the same. This explains why
they're known as Fermions, just like the class
of sub-atomic particles that obey
this same rather strange statistical law.
The others are named Bosons, after the class
of particles that rotate the once
to achieve their fearless symmetry.

A recipe for confusion? Only if
either party is not forewarned. For instance,
a Boson tailor or costumier
with a Fermion client for a fitting,
knows what to expect with 'Can you turn around?'
Equally, a Fermion tailor will need
nimble digits that can work twice as fast
to avoid keeping a Boson client waiting,
and be sensitive to the risk of giddiness.
An identification parade of Fermions
takes twice as long as when it's Bosons.

Medical investigations, including scans,
will need to factor in the rotation class.
Skating judges ensure a Fermion
isn't penalised in combination spins.

And it's not as if there is a rigid
dividing line between the two classes.
In certain conditions, such as severe cold,
a Fermion can flip class and go bosonic.
Turn up the heat, the double rotation's back.

Young aliens of either class often ask
what purpose is served by this difference.
Surely, life would be simpler, cleaner, neater,
with just one class, one elementary law.
'If you could wave a magic wand
that would affect no alien now living,
and thus eliminate this difference
in future generations, would you do so?'
Curiously, this question tends to be asked
more often by Boson children (and some adults).

Research has shown that alien life appears
to need both if it is to thrive. Besides,
an alien knows that while it's always tempting
to opt for any kind of uniformity,
experience of myriad other life forms
shows that only a fool would reach inside
some giant machine we hardly understand
and start yanking out the circuits.

God knows no mercy. Is there nothing
that does not assail the alien body
the longer it (just) survives? Some push
for shock wave treatment, hoping this will work.
It seems to have rather a high success rate
in problems affecting the extremities.

If, however, an alien has had enough
and fancies the ragged but happy life,
with or without benefit of shock waves,
the Gaugin-in-Tahiti option beckons,
minus the local sexual exploitation,
and any additional disease, of course.

Nothing worth spending any money on.
But no self-imposed restrictions either,
obsessive etiquette, ritualistic rules
of behaviour no alien need observe,
that are no sooner spoken than broken.
A rich tramp's life, no more, no less.

It's not only the skeleton (exo- or endo-)
that benefits from the balmy weather.
Alien mental health improves. Farewell
to insoles, walking sticks, replaced antennae,
the solace of 'Coffee is my only friend',
finding some meaning in one's suffering.

After Earthling composer Morton Feldman

Do not assume that aliens have no criminal histories.
Or that there is a gadget that wipes everything clean
from the record, that disappears all traces of data,
akin to a memory hole in the Ministry of Truth
for disposing of awkward, incriminating evidence,
sucked down a one-way chute to nothing happened.

There was that kidnapping business on Zog
with the former president held captive fifty-five days
before being found vaporised in an abandoned shuttle
with traces of sand and vegetables in its spacesuit.
Then there was the ritual cleansing of the Martian hives
as reconstructed by Professor Quatermass via telekinesis.

And what about the forced dispersal and deportation
of the Sirkazians of Alpha Ophiuci? Revisiting aliens
walk on the surface of the planet as if on eggshells,
pause in abandoned streets, point down to the stones,
and whisper, 'Can't you hear them? They're screaming!
Still screaming out from under the pavements!'

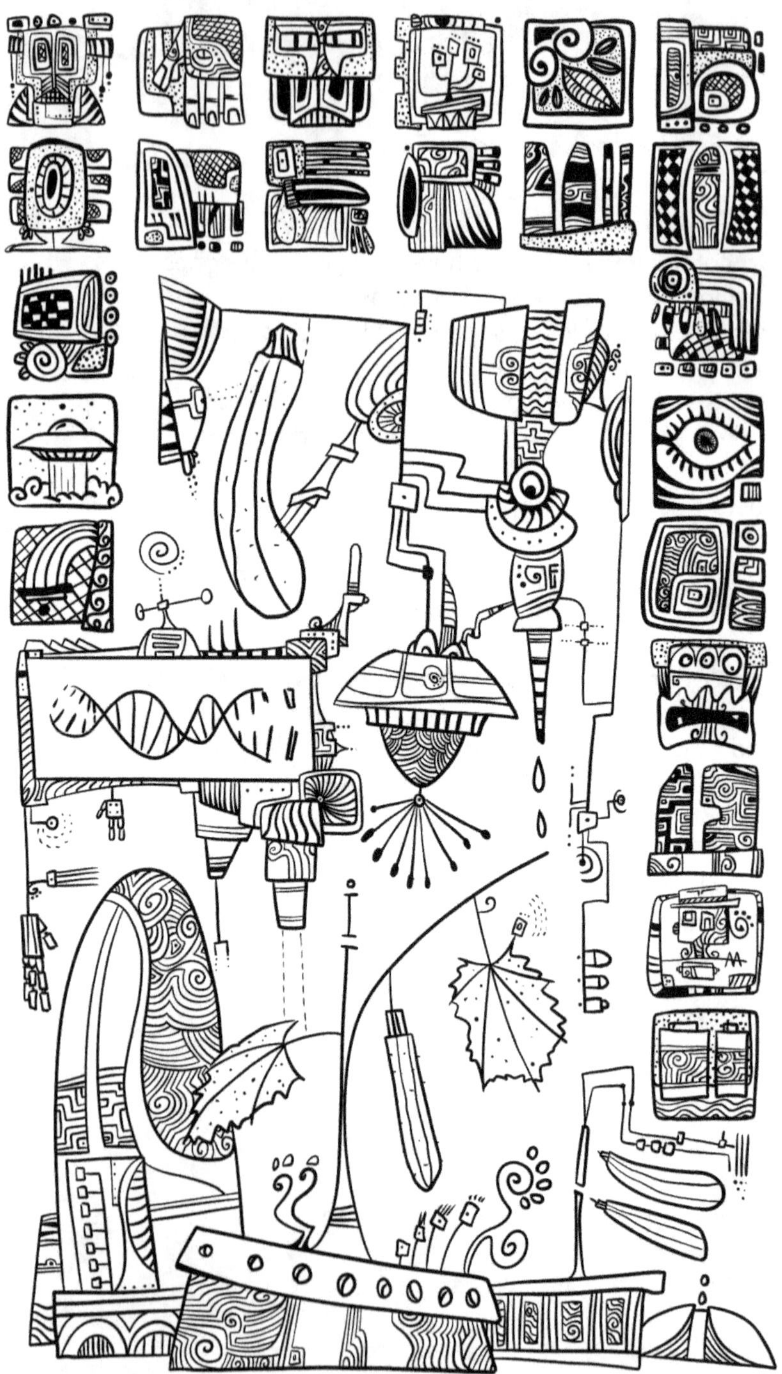

The alien had come across a pair,
abandoned on some godforsaken planet –
no one around as far as the eye could see –
gasping for H_2O, no shade, and wilting
under a pitiless yellow dwarf sun.

The alien did impromptu resuscitation
with some onboard equipment, after easing
the two plants out of the brown baked soil,
transporting what we presume were grateful creatures
to more hospitable climes and company.

Aliens know how to cultivate a friendship;
the least of it is reciprocation.
Plus, the alien wasn't a fool, it didn't expect
a thank-you note. It was enough these objects
shared their abundant secrets wordlessly.

By trial and not too much error the alien
discovered how to foster a family.
Each time one fruited, it marvelled at
the glossy green skin with speckled texture,
such a sweet contrast with its own jade rind.

'What's it called?' a curious visitor asked.
'I found it nameless, haven't the presumption
to confer one on it.' Friends soon began
to detect an obsession: 'They're only plants,
not even indigenous.' Alien silence.

'You know what they say about the ethics
or exotic species.' The alien was unmoved.

So, when the alien made this noise at night,
and gyrated in a way aligned to the poles,
those versed in alien mating rituals

began to suspect more was involved here
than innocent horticultural attention.
A guest came in and took a gourmet's sniff:
'Have you thought of trying one of these to eat?'
The alien sprayed its beer across the room.

Aliens have their distinct approach to therapy.
Naturally, some of the problems are specific to frequent flyers:
culture shock, déjà vu, or compassion fatigue
at the same vehement refusals
of beings to learn from experience or each other.

Any universal approach has long been abandoned.
Instead, there exists an evolving compendium,
'The Barefoot Alien's Manual', a survival guide
to fashions in therapy and ways to avoid it,
or at least avert the need for it.

Mental distress, of course, is no joke:
a state of mind (or no-mind), not a place to linger.
Aliens much prefer such expressions as
'My descent into psychosis'
or 'The other side of madness',

relying on nouns, verbs and adverbs of motion.
To do otherwise would be to suggest
that the state is less than temporary,
a disquieting notion and one at variance with
enlightened alien opinion.

The mighty Parnokios could bear it no longer;
like a fever consuming the hours of night and day
the living question possessed it.
Not staying to eat, it left its house before daybreak
arriving at the place where the most famous
Altairan philosopher lived, at an hour that,
by anyone's standards, was unseemly.
Ignoring civility, for such was its desperation,
it demanded an audience with the Wise One.
The servant replied that the Wise One was in the garden,
not to be disturbed, for this was the hour before morning
it gave over to solitary communion, such being the time
when Body, Mind and Nature were most likely to accord.
Parnokios would have none of it, and sent via the servant
the peremptory question, would stay and await an answer:
'Which must I follow, Wise One,
the way of the Spirit, or the way of the Body?
Unguided in my choice I must surely perish.'
The reply was reported by the servant
from the Wise One in its garden:
'Tell mighty Parnokios not to bother me with such nonsense.
I am absorbed (for the moment) body and soul
in the all-important activity of shitting.'

As told to Earthling playwright Carl Morse
who made it into 'Bruce Spruce'

An alien has an idea for a play.
It's this. The lights go up on a tree,
centre stage. The tree is not synthetic,
two metres in height for preference,
not ornamental and not evergreen.
Decidedly deciduous: the leaves
should be fellable, a plant to delight
any discerning horticulturist.
Enter an adult alien, gender flexible,
who approaches the tree, stops, looks and pulls
a leaf off, smells it, registers no smell,
drops it, and exits. Enter a second
alien with quadrupet on a leash.
Pet cocks a leg on the tree. Owner tugs pet.
Pause. Exeunt. Enter a romantically
entwined couple, genders as above.
They stop by the tree, disengage. One takes
out a knife, carves initials on the bark.
Exeunt. A succession of aliens enter
one by one, in pairs, or in small clusters,
each visit inflicting casual aggression
on the tree. Injuries are incremental
and may be creative. Actors can workshop
the concept: actions might include bark tearing,
an episode of throwing up, a daring dump,
snapping off a branch or two with one's claws,
waving a laser blaster at the base.
Suggested *coup de grâce*, incineration,
by a small phaser gun, for example.
Initial murmurs and twitching of seats

will give way to audible outrage,
albeit at this stage politely expressed.
Then a few silent exits, then more noisy.
Programmes brandished, with cries of 'Stop it! Now!'
A toffee pelted on-stage, then a shout
'Don't hit the tree!' puts a stop to further missiles.
Hubbub, debate, necks craned in all directions.
Finally, a brave alien (or possibly a plant,
not literally a plant, of course) storms the stage.
Aliens file over to the lighted space,
and form a cordon sanitaire around
the tree, protecting it from further insult.
Production team and the actors step aside.
The mêlée settles down, one finds a voice,
its unmiked presence quelling any fight.
The rights of the vulnerable, tormented,
ill-treated, huddled aliens everywhere,
of every living thing, are reasserted.
The tree, or what's been spared, is carried forth
with reverence into the street, up to the stars,
an emblem of those truths we have neglected.
The age of Alien Nation at an end.
And so the revolution will begin.

Unlike next year's Trollenberg Terror,
which is the genuine article,
this one is technically not an alien,
even if most of the boxes get a tick:
hideous radioactive mutant; summoned
from the future by a rogue experiment;
now on a mission to kidnap a scientist –

young white male American, of course –
as sperm donor saviour to revamp
the radioactive future's gene pool;
steals face of an unsuspecting nurse;
hypnotises with silver fingernails;
is implicated in a dead, four-eyed cat
dumped in a briefcase in a nearby swamp.

We know why the Terror's here, and how.
An exchange of tokens in the scientists' lab
begins the process: a statuette from them,
like Venus de Milo imagined by Duchamp;
a Phi Beta Kappa graduation key in return;
a coin from them with a Greek inscription
conveying the urgent message 'Save us'.

Is it then any wonder that the first words
addressed in person by the Terror,
to Victim No. 2, are also in Greek?
Terrors make the logical inference,
that a classical education isn't one
for bandying on trinkets. Best take care
what you send through time and space.

Criticism should not over-interpret
a filmic imagination of disaster.
But the premise is a serious one.
Consider: beings with spoiled identity,
maimed offspring of human greed and folly,
disqualified from social acceptance,
condemned to a life of wretchedness.

Who wouldn't resort to desperate measures
such as deception, hypnosis, mugging up
a dead foreign language, borrowing a face?
Admittedly, this last tactic does backfire.
Terrors, like aliens, know all too well
the unremitting reaction the second
they show their hand or claw: 'You're one of those freaks!'

As for the film's conclusion, once the Terror
has been despatched by a zillion volts,
that gifting uncontaminated blood
to the gulags of the Year 5000
will only open the floodgates to
an invading army of untouchables,
where have we heard that argument before?

Sartre was right, the aliens reflected.
What Earthlings tend to fear the most
in any science fiction alien
is a creature of energy and cunning
devoid of all human scruple.

This more or less describes to a T
the human being at war or in times
of scarcity. The film *Forbidden Planet*
made the same point as the Left Bank pundit.
No need to look beyond Paris or Altair IV.

An alien takes a leaf out of Wang Wei

Not to have heard the nightingale of the hundredth planet,
nor the distant bell sounding at the mouth of the petrified valley,

not to have seen the colours of so many sunsets,
so delicate they hardly register on lunar horizons,

to have counted fewer and fewer stars as a black hole approaches,
brushed actual dust from the ancient texts and watched motes flying,

taken a lute, and waited for the slow moons to climb,
and play by the peach stream where the Han are unknown …

And what has this being without occupation done?
It has passed an entire day behind a closed screen.

Even an alien has its melancholy moments.

It's said that those aliens lacking limbs –
with no legs and feet, extensor arms –
that literally want the art of manipulation,
are missing a trick.

A proboscis or antenna isn't quite the same
since sensors deal solely with information.
And whatever a tongue can do is short term.
The hand or claw, it's said,

holds up a kind of mirror to the self,
a paradigm of the capacity for objectivity,
as well as being an instrumental tool.
Go out on a limb?

How do aliens without seek self-knowledge, adventure?
Those that inhabit aerial and liquid environments
exploit their potential. While wings and tentacles
might count as limbs,

many a technology is created with fin or tail,
and coral polyps have founded civilisations.
As for the thing with mirrors, what need for those
when you've one all around you?

'That's it. Now, you're a thinly-disguised human being.
Sorry to say this, but you could pass for one of them.
The skin should be set in about an hour. We've sprayed it
with pheromones to throw Earth creatures off the scent.
You'll have several passports since we can't be certain
where you'll be dropped but it will be terra firma.
Remember, it's not just who you are but who you hate.'

'Feels more like thickly disguised to me. Disgusting.
A surface pH factor of less than 5: what use is that
against a strong alkali? Thank you for giving me
pheromones that smell of their vanilla and not their armpits.
The variety of colours ought to be its main benefit,
but this thought seems not to have occurred to them.
I'll say it again, carbon has a lot to answer for.'

Without killing the patient

Incise the integument
vertically down the abdomen.

Cut likewise the fascia.

Separate the rectus muscle,
hold back with retractors.

Remove with tweezers.

Try not to annoy it.

If life were that simple.

Before the discovery of vector drive
the only aliens capable of managing
less than superluminal motion
to travel to distant galaxies and back
were those of an extreme longevity
for whom the periods of time involved
posed no obstacles of any moment.

They were used to the long haul, outliving
other species, and immune to culture shock.
Not surprisingly, then, they were in demand
as cosmonauts and good-will ambassadors.
Previous careers as librarians, fact-checkers
and witnesses to historical events
were shucked in favour of derring-do.

Then, after many generations (common style),
and the advent of faster-than-light propulsion,
the spacesuit became an option for all.
The longeves found themselves out of a job,
superannuated, back at the checkout desk,
with all the time in the world – precisely
the commodity no longer called for.

Requests to become the ship's librarian
were politely declined. Some began memoirs
but abandoned these after volume seven thousand.
Others took to hosting steampunk conventions.
A few tried to conduct one last orbit of honour
but in the event this proved to take even longer
than a fading rock star's final farewell tour.

Chalk and cheese?
No, they are not:

one like this,
the other that,

of necessity,
by nature,

nothing in common,
properties fixed.

There are soft chalks,
there are hard cheeses.

Blue, green, orange,
yellow, red, brown:

no colour is owned
by chalk or cheese.

Chalks may wear down
in a single week,

some cheeses age
over many years.

In face of a vintage
classroom blackboard

a chalk may take
a vow of silence,

some cheeses even
squeak when you bite them.

Aliens are not spared the pangs of romance.
While the song has it that each alien is
a cosmonaut orbiting its beloved,
work does not favour light-year relationships.

That said, most aliens feel the urge
to give it a go, the once, before wiping
the final lines of primordial lyrics,
and opting for the unaccompanied lute.

One alien bucked the trend, however,
and kept its would-be parting memorandum.
'Read this? You shan't' – phrases that verged on hubris
in the message the alien had written thirty years back,

addressed in absentia, with said caveat,
to a former lover of whose present
whereabouts all interstellar searches
later proved to be ignorant. So far,

so predicted, even if the alien
would have been grateful for any sign
that had revoked its will, any pretext
for an update, amendment, or anything

challenging the blunt terms and conditions.
Re-reading it, the alien sighed. Unfinished business?
Unfinished grammar there was, perhaps.
An alien plays the hand life deals it.

Love was ever the prisoner of syntax.

Manifold are the methods of child-rearing
among the alien communities,
in terms of numbers of parents and others,
combinations of genders, or no gender,
length and intensity of parenting.
Some things are universally proscribed.
Infanticide, most will be relieved to hear,
is frowned upon. Few aliens abandon
their progeny on wind-swept satellites.
Even reptilian aliens maintain an interest
in life after egg. Methods can be reduced
to four types: seen and heard; seen but not heard;
heard but not seen; and neither seen nor heard.

Seen and Heard

One of the most popular.
The Cassiopeians set the trend. At birth
each child is given a parental monitor,
excreted from the mother's body.
No larger than a fly, this circulates
above the neonate, relaying sound and image
directly to either mother or father,
a literal helicopter parenting.
There's no risk of accidental inhalation
or ingestion because Cassiopeians
have no trachea or oesophagus.
Parents take turns to sleep and go off duty.
The living monitor follows the offspring
until the age of eighteen. It can be distracting
for both parent and child, especially in groups,
or if the child gets an urge for independence.
Children are known to swap or barter flies
(known as 'pulling the wool over your flies').

The end of continuous surveillance
is a rite of passage, acknowledged
as D-D-Day, 'Disappearance of the Drone'.
Many a parent heaves a sigh of relief
when it can put at least one fly to bed.

Seen but Not Heard

The Sagittarrians have this capacity –
the envy of many galaxies –
for closing off their ears at will to the sound
of their own particular infant.
Everything and everyone else is heard as normal.
A kind of auditory drawbridge
that provides the first line of defence
against pester power, tantrums and vengeful screams.
Children soon learn to recognise
the beatific look on their parent's face
that means the argument's been lost
or when the permitted number of questions
beginning 'Why?' has been exceeded.

Heard but Not Seen

One that's left field. The inhabitants
of Ursa Minor place their children
'under cover' in the form of tents
that obscure all visible body parts.
Unkind critics call it child espionage.
The child moves about, or usually stays still,
beneath its canopy, coloured light grey.
Routine caring activities are carried out

by 'reading' the child's body under its cloth,
by the lightest of touches, akin to Braille.
Children communicate verbally, by cooing.
Thus, adults exercise complete control
over information in and out of tents.
It's said this preserves a child's innocence
until it reaches adulthood, at which point
an alien emerges from its chrysalis,
and blinks wonderingly for the first time
at a world of sunlight and horizons,
mirrors and unmediated faces.
Some graduates initially go back under
or retain a fierce grip on their comfort blanket.
'Are you not curious to take a peek?'
and 'A child's body is nothing to fear'
might provide starting points for discussion,
a basis for gentle awareness-raising,
but this would run up against the policy
of non-interference in local alien customs.
So far, Ursa Minorans are unimpressed
by the indecent exposure, explicit gestures,
the jiving, back chat and inquisitive stares
of other aliens' children. They're upholding
the tent's beneficent necessity,
convinced it will catch on. It may be
a long wait. Definitely one to watch.

Neither Seen Nor Heard

A good example of this last is afforded
by the inhabitants of the planet Borealis.
They rely on smell and smell alone
to guide them to their offspring, and vice versa.
The dewy eye, the smile of recognition,

the attentive ping of the pinna,
the first part of the outer ear's anatomy
that reacts to sound or expresses emotion,
common to so many aliens, in their case
is replaced by a quiver or twitch of the nostril,
capable of registering a diapason
of the subtlest feelings and intentions,
the entire compass of parental moods.

We're always on the qui vive for messages.
Last night, for instance, an Earthling's dream
had absent parents, a red telephone,
and a call with them, to dispute the hour:
she had eleven, they insisted ten.
What was that all about? When she awoke
she had a buzzing in her left ear, a kind
of tinnitus. Was that significant?
'What would an alien make of this?'

No sooner had she said this to herself
than we realised she had lost the moment.
Like the more subtle kind of therapist,
we aliens do not offer interpretations,
least of all the deep-dive plunging kind,
or trip you up with 'Did you like your father?'
We would be more likely to suggest:
'Become the red phone: what brand are you?
What is your ring tone? What are you like to hold?'

The day it was announced the first aliens were to land,
the world's leaders were in a flutter. Who'd be first to greet them?
Once lots were drawn (and even that was controversial),
an agreed running order was established.
Imagine their consternation then, when the alien,
after the fanfares and formal introductions
(for the alien had done its homework and was multilingual),
and exchange of gifts (though what the alien handed out
bore no resemblance to anything living or dead),
explained it was half an alien.
It was quite customary to split journeys in this way.

'And when might we expect the other half?' one leader asked.
'That hasn't been decided,' the alien replied,
'you see, I never speak with one mind.'
This, and other such answers the alien willingly gave,
proved to be most unsatisfactory.
How could one negotiate with someone
who readily admitted its word was never final?
How could the treaty about undying friendship
and cooperation that had been drawn up
pass muster in the courts with half a signature?
How could someone's half a bond be trusted?

The Earth's media, initially gung ho, started
to have second thoughts about the business case.
Half an alien meant half the fee for exclusives,
but any sassy alien might insist on full pay
while giving half the time, making half the effort.
Most social media had no policy for half accounts,
went into meltdown with fake other half profiles.
Influencers, pundits and celebrities all vied
to come up with the most half-cocked phrases going:
half-hearted, too clever by half, half a mind to,
how the other half lives. The word soon grated.

In fact, there proved to be greater interest in
what the other half looked like, said and did.
Speculation was rife that the other half
was more dynamic, cool or cute, or richer:
alternatively, oppressed, abused or a survivor.
Was its identity stolen? Who'd speak for it?
Rival camps divided the nations. The 'other'
soon acquired a life, its own back story. Protests
and vigils were held for the silenced partner.
No point relying on the half in front of them,
all you would get at best was half-truths.

Eventually, people wearied of the uncertainty.
Nothing went viral anymore. The alien was told,
whichever half it was, in no uncertain terms,
to go back home, it was no longer welcome.
This would be difficult, the alien explained,
because it had travelled on only half a tank,
there wasn't enough to get even half-way back.
That's your problem, the world leaders said.
One thing they'd sussed out pretty quickly
was just how much these aliens have attitude.
Trouble was, they always saw the glass half empty.

Steve Cranfield is a poet, translator and educator living in London. His first collection of poetry, *Music for the Soviet Minister of Culture*, was published by Gay Men's Press in *Salt and Honey* (shared with fellow poet Martin Humphries). Gregory Woods wrote of the poet that 'he manages to combine his technical cool with the sensitivity of a seismograph. He sometimes seems to be kitted out with the poetic equivalent of X-ray specs' – a skill he would later put to good use in interpreting dictations from aliens. His *Keats's Anchovy* (2021) was praised by the writer and critic Paul Binding as 'an admirable blend of the deeply felt, the intensely thought, and the technically adventurous'. *Prospero's Cave*, a memoir in verse of the artist Peter Forster, appeared in 2022. His co-translation with Claudio Tedesco, funded by the Spanish Ministry of Culture, of poetry by the eminent Spanish writer Francisco Brines, *Of Purest Blue*, was published in 2010 (reprinted 2020). *The Creative University*, his full-length study of the literary critic F. R. Leavis, appeared in 2015.

www.stevecranfield.co.uk

Andrea Aste is a multimedia visionary artist and animator, published author and illustrator. His works have been exhibited worldwide in prestigious museums, including the Musée Grévin Paris, Montreal and Geneva and the Natural Science Museum in Turin, art galleries such as the Guildhall Gallery, London, and at acclaimed art events like the Venice Biennale (2015). In the world of Tarot and graphic novels, Aste is famous for his card decks and hybrid novels: *The Book of Shadows: An Alchemist's Story* (2023), *The Tarot of Light and Shadow* (2020) and *The Lost Code of Tarot* (2017). He illustrated and authored *Oracolarium* (2020), the first oracle deck whose cards come to life with augmented reality animations when seen with a mobile app. After his much-acclaimed work as set designer for the international stage performer Arturo Brachetti, Aste relocated his studio to the UK, further developing his unique techniques for live on-stage illustration and animation, including for the horror show *Shiver* (2021), in collaboration with Sinister Masterplan and performed at the Grant Museum of Zoology, London, and *Hide* (2023) presented at London's prestigious Vault Festival.

www.andreaaste.co.uk

THE END?

* 9 7 8 1 7 3 9 9 3 0 1 2 7 *